CHRISTINE HAGGINS

Prayers for Strengthening Relationships and Family

Nurturing Love, Restoring Harmony, and Building Lasting Connections

Copyright © 2023 by Christine Haggins

All rights reserved. No part of this publication may be reproduced, stored or transmitted in any form or by any means, electronic, mechanical, photocopying, recording, scanning, or otherwise without written permission from the publisher. It is illegal to copy this book, post it to a website, or distribute it by any other means without permission.

First edition

This book was professionally typeset on Reedsy. Find out more at reedsy.com

Contents

INTRODUCTION	vi
COMPANION GUIDE	x
CHAPTER 1: PRAYERS FOR SPOUSAL BOND	1
Prayer for a Strong and Loving Marriage	1
Prayer for Unity and Understanding	2
Prayer for Healing and Reconciliation	4
CHAPTER 2: PRAYERS FOR PARENT-CHILD RELATIONSHIPS	7
Prayer for Parental Guidance and Wisdom	7
Prayer for Nurturing a Healthy Parent-Child Bond	9
Prayer for Healing and Restoration in Parent-Child Relationships	11
CHAPTER 3: PRAYERS FOR SIBLING CONNECTIONS	13
Prayer for Sibling Unity and Support	13
Prayer for Healing Past Wounds	15
Prayer for Strengthening Sibling Relationships	18

CHAPTER 4: PRAYERS FOR EXTENDED FAMILY ... 21
  Prayer for Unity and Peace among Relatives ... 21
  Prayer for Reconciliation and Forgiveness ... 23
  Prayer for Strengthening Family Ties ... 26

CHAPTER 5: PRAYERS FOR FRIENDS AND COMPANIONS ... 27
  Prayer for True and Faithful Friendships ... 27
  Prayer for Reconciliation and Renewed Connections ... 29
  Prayer for Blessings upon Friends ... 32

CHAPTER 6: PRAYERS FOR HEALING BROKEN RELATIONSHIPS ... 35
  Prayer for Restoration and Healing in Broken Relationships ... 35
  Prayer for Letting Go of Resentment and Anger ... 37
  Prayer for Reconciliation and Restoration ... 41

CHAPTER 7: PRAYERS FOR BUILDING HEALTHY COMMUNICATION ... 45
  Prayer for Open and Honest Communication ... 45
  Prayer for Listening and Understanding ... 47
  Prayer for Resolving Conflicts with Love and Grace ... 50

CHAPTER 8: PRAYERS FOR STRENGTHENING PARENTING SKILLS	54
Prayer for Patience and Wisdom in Parenting	54
Prayer for Nurturing a Healthy Parent-Child Relationship	56
Prayer for Guidance and Strength in Parenting Challenges	59
CHAPTER 9: PRAYERS FOR BLENDED FAMILIES	62
Prayer for Unity and Harmony in Blended Families	62
Prayer for Love and Acceptance among Stepfamily Members	65
Prayer for Strength and Guidance in Navigating the Challenges of Blended Families	67
CONCLUSION	71

INTRODUCTION

Welcome to "Prayers for Strengthening Relationships and Family: Nurturing Love, Restoring Harmony, and Building Lasting Connections." In this heartfelt collection of prayers, we embark on a journey to enhance and cultivate the most cherished bonds in our lives – our relationships and our families.

Relationships are the foundation of our existence, shaping who we are and how we navigate through life. Whether it's the bond between spouses, the connection between parents and children, the dynamics among siblings, or the friendships we hold dear, our relationships play a vital role in our happiness, growth, and overall well-being.

Yet, we are all aware that relationships can be complex and challenging. They require intentional effort, understanding, forgiveness, and love to thrive. It is in these moments that prayer becomes a powerful tool, providing solace, guidance, and healing.

Through prayer, we invite the divine presence into our relationships, seeking divine wisdom and intervention to nurture love, restore harmony, and build lasting connections.

In this book, you will find a collection of prayers designed to address various aspects of relationships and family dynamics. Each prayer is carefully crafted to touch upon the unique challenges and joys that accompany these sacred bonds. It is our hope that these prayers will serve as a source of inspiration, encouragement, and transformation in your own relationships and family life.

As you journey through the chapters, you will discover prayers for strengthening the spousal bond, nurturing parent-child relationships, fostering harmony among siblings, building connections with extended family, cherishing friendships, healing broken relationships, and navigating the complexities of blended families. Additionally, you will find prayers that focus on communication, forgiveness, understanding, and the development of healthy parenting skills.

The power of prayer lies not only in its ability to transform our own hearts but also in its potential to transform the relationships we hold dear. As we surrender our hopes, fears, and desires to the Divine, we open ourselves to divine guidance, healing, and restoration. Through prayer, we create space for love to flourish, for understanding to deepen, and for connections to grow stronger.

It is our prayer that this book will provide you with the language and inspiration to express your deepest desires, concerns, and gratitude to God. May these prayers become a companion on your journey, offering comfort during challenges, guidance in decision-making, and celebration in moments of joy. May they serve as a reminder that you are not alone in your quest to strengthen your relationships and build a loving family.

May your relationships be nourished by the grace of God, and may His love flow abundantly through your interactions, bringing harmony, joy, and lasting connections. As you engage in these prayers, open your heart to the transformative power of divine intervention and experience the beauty of strengthened relationships and family bonds.

May these prayers be a catalyst for growth, healing, and love in your life. May they ignite a spark of hope and inspire you to invest in the sacred connections that shape your world. Together, let us embark on this journey of prayer and discover the wonders that await us in strengthening relationships and building a strong, loving family.

With gratitude and anticipation,

Christine Haggins

COMPANION GUIDE

As you journey through the different prayers in this book, you might want to keep a journal close to pen down revelations and personal request.

This Prayer Request Journal specifically made for this purpose is all you need.

CHAPTER 1: PRAYERS FOR SPOUSAL BOND

Prayer for a Strong and Loving Marriage

Loving God, we come before you with grateful hearts, acknowledging that you are the source of love and the foundation of every strong marriage. We pray for our union, that it may be rooted in your unfailing love and guided by your wisdom.

Grant us the strength to nurture our relationship with kindness, compassion, and patience. Help us to see each other through your eyes, embracing each other's strengths and accepting each other's flaws. May our love for one another grow deeper each day, reflecting the selfless love of Christ.

Guide our words and actions, that they may be filled

with grace and understanding. Teach us to prioritize our commitment to one another, to be intentional in our communication, and to make space for both unity and individual growth. Give us the courage to confront challenges together, with open hearts and a willingness to forgive.

Lord, protect our marriage from any external forces that seek to undermine our bond. Shield us from resentment, selfishness, and the temptations that can lead us astray. Help us to continually choose love, even in the midst of disagreement or difficulty.

We pray for your divine presence in our home, that it may be a sanctuary of peace, joy, and laughter. May our marriage be a testimony of your faithfulness and a reflection of your love to those around us. Use our union to bring glory to your name and inspire others to seek a strong and loving marriage.

In Jesus' name, we pray. Amen.

Prayer for Unity and Understanding

Gracious God, we thank you for the gift of unity in our marriage. We recognize that unity is not merely the absence of conflict but the presence of understanding, empathy, and shared goals. Today, we come before you, seeking your guidance and grace to foster a deeper sense of unity in our relationship.

Help us to listen to one another with open hearts and open minds. Grant us the ability to truly hear and understand each other's hopes, dreams, and concerns. Teach us to prioritize our unity above individual desires and preferences, seeking to build a life together that reflects your divine purpose.

Lord, when disagreements arise, grant us the humility to seek common ground and find solutions that honor both of our perspectives. Fill our hearts with love and compassion, enabling us to empathize with each other's experiences and extend grace in moments of tension.

May our unity be a witness to your power and love. Use our relationship to inspire others to seek harmony and understanding in their own marriages. Let our union be a source of strength and support, demonstrating the beauty of two lives joined together in pursuit of a common purpose.

Lord, we commit our marriage to you, trusting that you will help us cultivate unity and understanding. With you as our guide, we know that nothing is impossible. We invite you into the intimate spaces of our hearts and relationship, knowing that you are the ultimate source of unity and harmony.

In Jesus' name, we pray. Amen.

Prayer for Healing and Reconciliation

Loving God, we bring before you our marriage, seeking your healing touch and the power of reconciliation. We acknowledge that every relationship encounters hardships and that we, too, have faced our share of trials. Today, we come before you with humble hearts, asking for your divine intervention.

Lord, we pray for healing where wounds have been inflicted. Heal the pain caused by hurtful words, misunderstandings, and broken promises. Restore trust where it has been shattered and grant us the grace to extend forgiveness to one another.

Guide us on the path of reconciliation, that we may rebuild what has been damaged. Help us to let go of past hurts and focus on the possibilities of renewal and restoration. Grant us the courage to have difficult conversations with love and respect, and the wisdom to find common ground and reach a place of understanding.

Lord, we surrender our egos and pride at your feet, knowing that true healing and reconciliation can only come through your grace. Soften our hearts and help us to see each other through your eyes of compassion. Give us the strength to be vulnerable and transparent, sharing our deepest fears and hopes as we work towards healing.

Pour out your love upon us, Lord, and fill our hearts with your peace. May your Holy Spirit guide us in every step of our journey towards reconciliation. Help us to cultivate an environment of forgiveness and grace, where we can grow together in love and understanding.

We pray for your divine intervention in our marriage, knowing that with you, all things are possible. Bring healing to our relationship and make us whole again. Restore the joy and intimacy we once shared, and let our love for one another be a testament to your transforming power.

May our marriage become a beacon of hope for others who are experiencing brokenness, reminding them that healing and reconciliation are within their reach. Use our journey to inspire others to seek healing in their own relationships and to trust in your ability to mend what is broken.

We surrender our marriage to you, Lord, and place it in your loving hands. Heal us, restore us, and renew us according to your perfect plan. In your holy name, we pray. Amen.

CHAPTER 2: PRAYERS FOR PARENT-CHILD RELATIONSHIPS

Prayer for Parental Guidance and Wisdom

Gracious God, we come before you as parents, acknowledging our need for your guidance and wisdom in raising our children. You have entrusted us with the precious gift of parenthood, and we humbly seek your help in navigating this sacred responsibility.

Grant us discernment and insight as we make decisions that shape the lives of our children. Help us to lead by example, demonstrating the values of love, integrity, and compassion. Strengthen our ability to set healthy boundaries and provide a nurturing environment where our children can thrive.

Lord, we pray for your wisdom to understand each child's unique needs, talents, and struggles. Give us the patience and empathy required to meet them where they are and guide them towards their full potential. Help us to be attentive listeners and supportive mentors, offering guidance with gentleness and understanding.

We surrender our worries and fears about parenting to you, O Lord. Fill us with confidence and trust in your divine plan for our children's lives. Help us to release our desire for control and embrace the truth that they ultimately belong to you. Grant us the wisdom to balance discipline and freedom, allowing our children to learn and grow while providing a safe and nurturing space for them to flourish.

May our words and actions as parents be filled with grace and love. Give us the strength to apologize when we make mistakes and to model humility and forgiveness. Help us to build strong bonds with our children, nurturing relationships built on trust, respect, and open communication.

Lord, bless our role as parents and fill us with your divine wisdom. Surround our children with your protective love and guidance. May they grow up to be individuals who reflect your character and positively impact the world around them.

In Jesus' name, we pray. Amen.

Prayer for Nurturing a Healthy Parent-Child Bond

Heavenly Father, we come before you with hearts full of gratitude for the gift of our children. We recognize that the parent-child bond is a sacred connection, one that has the power to shape lives and leave a lasting impact.

Lord, we pray for the grace to nurture a healthy and loving bond with our children. Help us to create an environment where they feel valued, accepted, and unconditionally loved. Teach us to celebrate their uniqueness and encourage their dreams, providing a firm foundation from which they can explore the world.

Grant us the patience and understanding to truly see our children for who they are. Help us to cultivate deep connections through meaningful conversations, shared experiences, and quality time spent together. May our interactions be filled with joy, laughter, and moments of deep connection that strengthen our bond.

Lord, guide us in the art of active listening, that we may truly hear the concerns, hopes, and fears of our children. Give us the wisdom to offer comfort and support when they face challenges, and the discernment to provide gentle guidance when they navigate life's uncertainties.

Help us to be present in their lives, to witness their growth, and to celebrate their achievements. Let us be their pillars of support and their safe haven in times of distress. Grant us the ability to recognize and affirm their unique gifts and talents, fostering an environment where they can flourish and thrive.

We recognize that our role as parents is a sacred privilege and responsibility. Help us to embrace this journey wholeheartedly, surrendering our own expectations and desires for our children's lives. May our love be unconditional, our guidance gentle, and our support unwavering.

Lord, we commit our parent-child relationships into your loving care. Guide us, teach us, and empower us to be the parents our children need. May our bond grow stronger with each passing day, and may our love for one another be a reflection of your divine love.

Prayer for Healing and Restoration in Parent-Child Relationships

Merciful God, we bring before you our parent-child relationships, recognizing that they are not always immune to difficulties and brokenness. We acknowledge that there may be wounds, misunderstandings, or strained connections that require your healing touch. Today, we seek your intervention, Lord, to bring about healing and restoration in our relationships.

Father, we lift up to you any hurts or pain that exist between us and our children. We ask for your healing power to mend what is broken, to mend relationships strained by conflict, and to bring reconciliation where there is division. Help us to let go of past grievances and to embrace forgiveness, understanding that it is through your grace that true healing can occur.

Grant us the courage to initiate conversations that lead to reconciliation and understanding. Guide our words and actions, that they may be filled with love, humility, and the desire for restoration. Help us to listen with open hearts and to seek to understand the perspectives of our children. Give us the wisdom to address any underlying issues and to work towards resolutions that honor both parties involved.

Lord, we pray for your healing touch to bring restoration to the broken bonds between parents and children. Pour out your love and grace upon us, softening hearts and opening doors for reconciliation. Help us to rebuild trust and create a safe space where honesty, vulnerability, and forgiveness can flourish.

In moments of difficulty, grant us the strength to persevere and to never give up on the potential for healing. Remind us that your love is capable of redeeming any brokenness and that reconciliation is possible through your power.

We commit our parent-child relationships to you, Lord, surrendering them into your loving care. We trust that you have a plan for our relationships, and we ask for your guidance and wisdom in navigating the path towards healing. Restore what has been lost, heal what has been wounded, and mend what has been broken, so that our relationships may be a testimony to your transformative love.

In the name of Jesus, we pray. Amen.

CHAPTER 3: PRAYERS FOR SIBLING CONNECTIONS

Prayer for Sibling Unity and Support

Loving God, we come before you with grateful hearts for the gift of siblings. We recognize that sibling relationships hold a unique place in our lives, offering us companionship, support, and a shared journey through life. Today, we lift up our siblings to you and ask for your blessings upon our connections.

Lord, we pray for unity and harmony among siblings. Help us to cultivate a spirit of love, understanding, and acceptance within our relationships. Teach us to appreciate the differences that make each sibling unique and to embrace the bond that ties us together as family.

Grant us the grace to be a source of support for one another. Help us to be there in times of joy and celebration, rejoicing in each other's successes. Give us the empathy and compassion to be present in times of sorrow and challenge, offering a listening ear, a comforting presence, and a helping hand.

Lord, we acknowledge that sibling relationships can be complex and prone to conflicts. We ask for your guidance and wisdom in navigating any disagreements or misunderstandings that may arise. Help us to communicate with kindness and respect, seeking resolution and understanding rather than division.

We pray for your healing touch upon any past wounds that may have strained our relationships. Grant us the humility and courage to seek forgiveness and extend forgiveness to one another. Heal the hurts and scars that may linger, replacing them with a renewed sense of love and unity.

May our sibling relationships be a reflection of your unconditional love, O Lord. Help us to build a strong foundation of trust, loyalty, and mutual support. Empower us to be each other's biggest cheerleaders, encouraging and inspiring one another to reach our full potential.

We commit our sibling connections into your hands, Lord. Bless our relationships with love, understanding, and unity. Strengthen the bonds that hold us together and help us to cherish the gift of siblingship. May our relationships bring joy, growth, and a sense of belonging to each of us.

In the name of Jesus, we pray. Amen.

Prayer for Healing Past Wounds

Compassionate God, we come before you with heavy hearts, acknowledging the wounds and hurts that may exist within our sibling relationships. We recognize that the journey of siblingship is not immune to pain and brokenness. Today, we seek your healing touch, Lord, to mend the wounds of the past and bring restoration to our relationships.

Father, we lift up to you any hurts, resentments, or misunderstandings that have caused division between us and our siblings. We ask for your divine intervention to heal the wounds that have left scars on our hearts. Pour out your mercy and grace upon us, washing away the pain and bitterness that may have taken root.

Grant us the courage to confront our past hurts and

to seek reconciliation with our siblings. Help us to engage in honest and vulnerable conversations, where we can express our feelings, listen to one another's perspectives, and find a path towards forgiveness and healing. Give us the wisdom to let go of grudges, to release the burden of resentment, and to embrace the power of reconciliation.

Lord, we recognize that healing may take time and require effort from all parties involved. We pray for patience, understanding, and a willingness to extend grace to one another. Help us to see beyond our differences and to focus on the bond of love that exists between siblings.

Guide us in the process of rebuilding trust and restoring our sibling connections. Help us to sow seeds of kindness, encouragement, and support in our interactions. May our words and actions reflect the desire for healing and restoration, nurturing an atmosphere of love, empathy, and acceptance.

We surrender our wounded sibling relationships to you, Lord, knowing that you are the ultimate healer and reconciler. We trust in your power to bring beauty out of brokenness and to transform our relationships with our siblings.

..., we pray for the strength to let go of past grievances and to extend forgiveness to our siblings. Help us to release any lingering resentment or bitterness, replacing it with a heart that is open to reconciliation and restoration. Grant us the humility to acknowledge our own faults and shortcomings, recognizing that we all make mistakes and are in need of your grace.

We ask for your healing presence to mend the fractures within our sibling relationships. Pour out your love and understanding upon us, enabling us to see one another through compassionate eyes. Heal the wounds that have caused distance, and help us to rebuild bridges of trust, respect, and affection.

May our journey towards healing be marked by humility, patience, and a commitment to growth. Give us the courage to have difficult conversations, to listen with empathy, and to seek understanding. Help us to find common ground and to appreciate the unique qualities and gifts that each sibling brings to the relationship.

Lord, we invite you into the process of restoration. Guide our steps, offer us wisdom, and shower us with your love as we embark on this journey of healing. May our sibling relationships become a testament to your transformative power, demonstrating the beauty of reconciliation and forgiveness.

We trust in your faithfulness, O Lord, to mend what is broken and to restore what has been lost. We place our hope in your ability to bring healing and wholeness to our sibling connections. Strengthen us as we seek to build bridges, nurture love, and cultivate lasting bonds.

In the name of Jesus, our ultimate healer, we pray. Amen.

Prayer for Strengthening Sibling Relationships

Heavenly Father,

I come before You today with a prayer for the strengthening of sibling relationships. You have blessed us with the gift of family, and within that family, we have brothers and sisters who share a special bond. However, Lord, sometimes this bond becomes strained, and conflicts arise that threaten to disrupt the harmony and love between siblings.

I lift up to You my relationship with my siblings, recognizing the importance of a strong and healthy connection. I ask for Your guidance and intervention in resolving any conflicts, misunderstandings, or resentments that may exist between us. Help us to communicate with love and understanding, to listen with open hearts, and to seek reconciliation when disagreements arise.

Lord, I pray for unity among siblings. May we support and encourage one another, celebrating each other's successes and offering comfort and strength in times of need. Teach us to appreciate the unique qualities and gifts that each sibling brings to our lives, and to embrace our differences with respect and love.

Please heal any wounds or hurts that have been inflicted upon us or that we have caused one another. Grant us the grace to forgive and to seek forgiveness, recognizing that forgiveness is a powerful catalyst for healing and restoration. Help us to let go of past grievances and to build a future based on love, forgiveness, and mutual respect.

Lord, I ask that You fill our hearts with empathy and compassion for one another. Give us the ability to see beyond our own perspectives and to genuinely understand and empathize with the experiences and emotions of our siblings. May we be quick to extend grace, patience, and kindness, nurturing a bond of love that withstands the test of time.

I also pray for the strengthening of our shared faith. Help us to grow closer to You as we support and encourage one another in our spiritual journeys. May our faith be a unifying force that deepens our bond as siblings and brings us closer to You.

Thank You, Lord, for the gift of siblings and the potential for beautiful relationships. I trust in Your power to bring healing, restoration, and unity among us. May our sibling relationships be a source of joy, love, and support, reflecting Your perfect love for us.

In the name of Jesus, I pray. Amen.

CHAPTER 4: PRAYERS FOR EXTENDED FAMILY

Prayer for Unity and Peace among Relatives

Gracious God, we come before you with grateful hearts for the gift of extended family. We recognize that our relatives play a significant role in shaping our lives and contributing to our sense of belonging. Today, we lift up our extended family members to you and ask for your blessings upon our relationships.

Lord, we pray for unity and peace among our relatives. Help us to foster an atmosphere of love, understanding, and respect within our extended family circles. We acknowledge that diverse personalities, backgrounds, and perspectives can sometimes lead to conflicts and misunderstandings. Grant us the wisdom and patience to navigate these differences with grace and compassion.

Instill within us a spirit of empathy and a willingness to listen to one another. Help us to appreciate the unique contributions and strengths that each family member brings to our collective tapestry. May we celebrate our diversity and find common ground that strengthens our bonds.

Lord, we recognize that extended family relationships can sometimes be strained due to various circumstances. We pray for healing in relationships that have been fractured or distant. Soften hearts, Lord, and open doors for reconciliation and restoration. Help us to mend the broken bonds and rebuild trust where it has been lost.

Grant us the courage to initiate conversations that promote understanding and bridge any gaps that exist. Help us to communicate with kindness, empathy, and a desire to build stronger connections. May our words and actions reflect our commitment to maintaining healthy and loving relationships within our extended family.

We ask for your guidance, Lord, in navigating the complexities of extended family dynamics. Grant us wisdom in knowing when to extend grace, when to speak up, and when to offer support. Teach us to prioritize forgiveness and reconciliation, knowing that these are essential ingredients for nurturing lasting bonds.

Lord, we commit our extended family relationships into your hands. Bless us with unity, peace, and love that surpasses any disagreements or differences. Help us to cherish the precious moments we share, to create lasting memories, and to build a legacy of love and connection for generations to come.

In the name of Jesus, who unites us as one family, we pray. Amen.

Prayer for Reconciliation and Forgiveness

Heavenly Father, we humbly come before you with hearts burdened by strained relationships within our extended family. We acknowledge that misunderstandings, conflicts, and hurtful words or actions can cause division and distance among relatives. Today, we seek your divine intervention to bring about reconciliation and forgiveness.

Lord, we confess any role we have played in perpetuating discord within our extended family. We ask for your forgiveness for any words spoken, actions taken, or grudges held that have hindered the restoration of our relationships. Give us the humility to admit our mistakes and the courage to seek reconciliation.

We pray for the healing of wounded hearts and the mending of broken bonds. Soften the hearts of our family members, Lord, and help us to see beyond our differences and shortcomings. Grant us the grace to extend forgiveness to one another, following the example of your unconditional love and forgiveness towards us.

Guide us, Lord, in the process of reconciliation. Help us to engage in honest and respectful conversations, where we can express our feelings, listen to one another's perspectives, and seek understanding. Give us the wisdom to let go of past hurts, to release the burden of resentment, and to embrace the power of forgiveness.

Lord, we ask for your peace to reign within our extended family. Dispel any bitterness, anger, or grudges that may have taken root in our hearts. Replace them with your love, understanding, and a genuine desire for reconciliation. Help us to restore trust, rebuild bridges, and create an environment where love and harmony can flourish.

We pray for divine intervention, Lord, knowing that only through your grace can true reconciliation be achieved. Pour out your healing balm upon our extended family, bringing restoration and wholeness to our relationships. May forgiveness flow freely, and may the wounds of the past be transformed into opportunities for growth and deeper connection.

Father, we recognize that reconciliation requires effort and a willingness to let go of pride and ego. Grant us the strength to initiate conversations, to seek understanding, and to extend the hand of forgiveness. Help us to put aside our differences and focus on the love that binds us as family.

Teach us, Lord, to foster an atmosphere of compassion, empathy, and patience within our extended family. Give us the ability to see one another through your eyes, to acknowledge our shared humanity, and to embrace each other's imperfections. Help us to offer support, encouragement, and unconditional love as we journey together.

Lord, we pray for a fresh start in our extended family relationships. May the past be buried, and may new beginnings be embraced with hope and optimism.

Help us to create lasting memories filled with joy, laughter, and shared experiences. May our family gatherings be marked by unity, love, and genuine connections.

We entrust our extended family ties to you, Lord, knowing that you are the ultimate reconciler and healer. Guide us on this journey of forgiveness and restoration, and lead us into a future where our extended family is a source of strength, support, and unconditional love.

In the name of Jesus, who taught us to love one another as family, we pray. Amen.

Prayer for Strengthening Family Ties

Heavenly Father,

I come before You today with a prayer for the strengthening of family ties. You have designed the family as a foundation of love and support, and I recognize the importance of strong and healthy relationships within my family. Lord, I ask for Your guidance and intervention in nurturing and deepening the bonds that unite us as a family.

CHAPTER 5: PRAYERS FOR FRIENDS AND COMPANIONS

Prayer for True and Faithful Friendships

Gracious God, we thank you for the gift of friends and companions who journey with us through life. Today, we come before you, seeking your blessings upon our friendships. We long for true and faithful friendships that reflect your love, grace, and wisdom.

Lord, we pray for genuine connections rooted in trust, loyalty, and mutual respect. Surround us with friends who encourage, support, and inspire us to grow in our faith and character. Help us to cultivate friendships that are built on a foundation of shared values, shared joys, and shared sorrows.

Guide us, Lord, in choosing our friends wisely. Help us to discern those individuals who will uplift and challenge us, who will walk beside us in both good times and bad. Give us the wisdom to recognize toxic relationships and the courage to distance ourselves from negative influences.

We pray for the deepening of existing friendships. May we invest time, effort, and care in nurturing these precious connections. Help us to be attentive listeners, compassionate supporters, and faithful companions to our friends. May our relationships be marked by vulnerability, authenticity, and mutual growth.

Lord, we ask for your grace in resolving conflicts and misunderstandings that may arise within our friendships. Grant us the humility to admit our mistakes, the openness to receive correction, and the willingness to extend forgiveness. Help us to practice grace and patience, understanding that friendships require effort, understanding, and a commitment to unity.

Bless our friendships, Lord, with joy, laughter, and shared experiences. May we celebrate one another's successes, comfort one another in times of sorrow, and provide a safe space for vulnerability and authenticity. Help us to foster a sense of belonging, acceptance, and belongingness within our circle of friends.

Above all, Lord, may our friendships be a reflection of your love. Teach us to love one another selflessly, to bear one another's burdens, and to spur one another on towards love and good deeds. May our friendships be a source of strength, encouragement, and accountability as we navigate the journey of life together.

In the name of Jesus, our truest friend and companion, we pray. Amen.

Prayer for Reconciliation and Renewed Connections

Heavenly Father, we come before you with heavy hearts burdened by broken friendships and strained connections. We recognize that friendships, like any relationship, can experience challenges and fractures. Today, we humbly seek your intervention to bring about reconciliation and renewed connections among our friends.

Lord, we acknowledge the pain that comes with fractured friendships. We lift up to you those relationships that have suffered from misunderstandings, disagreements, or hurtful words and actions. We ask for your healing touch to mend the brokenness and to restore what has been lost.

Grant us the courage to initiate conversations and extend the olive branch of reconciliation. Help us to listen with empathy, to speak with kindness, and to seek understanding. Soften hearts, Lord, and remove the walls of pride and stubbornness that prevent reconciliation. May forgiveness flow freely, and may past hurts be replaced with healing and restoration.

We pray for wisdom and discernment in discerning which friendships are worth pursuing and which ones may be toxic or unhealthy. Guide us, Lord, in choosing the right path for our friendships. Help us to discern when it is necessary to let go of certain relationships and when it is worth investing time and effort into rebuilding connections.

We trust in your sovereign plan, Lord, knowing that you can bring beauty out of brokenness. We surrender our broken friendships into your hands and ask for your divine intervention. Help us to release any bitterness, resentment, or unforgiveness, replacing them with hearts filled with grace, love, and understanding and renew the bonds that have been strained. Grant us the courage to reach out to our friends, to apologize for our shortcomings, and to extend forgiveness where it is needed.

Lord, we pray for reconciliation not only in our broken friendships but also in our own hearts. Help us to examine ourselves and identify areas where we may have contributed to the breakdown of these relationships. Give us the humility to acknowledge our faults and the willingness to make amends.

We lift up to you, Lord, those friends with whom we have lost touch or grown distant. Restore the connections that have faded over time. Rekindle the flames of friendship and guide us back to a place of closeness and understanding. Help us to bridge the gaps and rebuild the trust that may have been eroded.

Father, we also ask for your guidance in discerning when it may be necessary to let go of friendships that are no longer serving our growth and well-being. Give us the strength to release toxic relationships and surround ourselves with friends who uplift, inspire, and support us. Help us to prioritize our emotional and spiritual well-being while maintaining compassion and grace.

We pray for your blessings upon our friendships, Lord. May they be marked by love, trust, and mutual respect. Grant us the ability to celebrate one another's victories, to offer a listening ear in times of struggle, and to be a source of encouragement and inspiration. Help us to cultivate friendships that stand the test of time and bring joy and fulfillment to our lives.

Lord, we commit our friendships into your hands, knowing that you are the ultimate healer and restorer. Guide us on the path of reconciliation and renewal, and may our friendships reflect your love and grace. May they be a testament to your transformative power in our lives.

In the name of Jesus, our friend and redeemer, we pray. Amen.

Prayer for Blessings upon Friends

Gracious Lord,

Today, I lift up my dear friends to You and offer this prayer for blessings upon their lives. Thank You for the gift of friendship, for the beautiful souls You have brought into my life to walk alongside me, support me, and bring joy and companionship.

Heavenly Father, I ask that You pour out Your abundant blessings upon my friends. May Your love and favor encompass them in every area of their lives. Grant them good health, both physically and emotionally, so that they may thrive and experience vitality in their daily endeavors.

I pray for blessings upon their relationships, whether with their families, significant others, or friends. May their connections be filled with love, understanding, and mutual support. Strengthen the bonds they share, fostering unity, trust, and harmony. Surround them with healthy and uplifting relationships that contribute to their overall well-being.

Lord, bless my friends with wisdom and guidance in their decision-making. Grant them clarity of mind and discernment as they navigate life's challenges and opportunities. May they have the courage to pursue their dreams, using their unique gifts and talents to make a positive impact in the world.

I also pray for their financial well-being. Provide for their needs, open doors of opportunities, and bless their endeavors. May they experience financial stability and abundance, allowing them to live generously and contribute to the needs of others.

Above all, I pray for their spiritual journey. Draw them closer to You, Lord, and deepen their relationship with You. May they experience Your presence and peace in their lives, finding comfort and strength in times of difficulty and rejoicing in times of joy. Help them to grow in faith, to trust in Your plans for them, and to walk in alignment with Your will.

Finally, I ask for Your protection over my friends. Guard them against harm, danger, and temptation. Surround them with Your angels and keep them safe in all their ways.

Lord, I commit my friends into Your loving care, knowing that You are the source of every good and perfect gift. Thank You for the blessings they bring into my life, and I ask that You multiply those blessings in their lives.

In Jesus' name, I pray. Amen.

CHAPTER 6: PRAYERS FOR HEALING BROKEN RELATIONSHIPS

Prayer for Restoration and Healing in Broken Relationships

Heavenly Father, we come before you with heavy hearts, burdened by broken relationships that have caused us pain and sorrow. We acknowledge that relationships can falter, leaving us feeling wounded and disconnected. Today, we humbly seek your divine intervention for restoration and healing in these broken relationships.

Lord, you are the ultimate healer and restorer. We bring before you the relationships that have been fractured, asking for your transformative touch to mend what has been broken. We pray for reconciliation, understanding, and a restoration of trust and love. Pour out your grace and mercy upon these broken relationships, Lord, and guide us towards reconciliation.

Grant us the wisdom to know how to mend these broken bonds. Give us the courage to initiate conversations, to listen with empathy, and to speak with love and understanding. Help us to acknowledge our own faults and shortcomings, taking responsibility for our part in the breakdown of these relationships. Fill our hearts with humility, Lord, and remove any barriers that hinder forgiveness and reconciliation.

We pray for healing, both for ourselves and for the individuals with whom we have strained relationships. Bring healing to the wounds of the past, soothing the pain and hurt that have caused division. Soften hardened hearts, Lord, and replace bitterness with forgiveness, anger with compassion, and resentment with love. Help us to release grudges and to embrace the possibility of restoration and reconciliation.

Lord, we surrender our broken relationships into your hands. We trust in your wisdom and perfect timing. Guide us on the path of healing, showing us when to persist and when to let go. Grant us the patience and perseverance to seek healing, even when it feels challenging or impossible.

We pray for your divine intervention, Lord, believing that you are able to restore what is broken and to heal what is wounded. Fill us with hope, peace, and a renewed sense of purpose as we navigate the journey of healing broken relationships.

In the name of Jesus, the ultimate reconciler and healer, we pray. Amen.

Prayer for Letting Go of Resentment and Anger

Gracious God, we come before you burdened by feelings of resentment and anger towards those who have hurt us. We acknowledge that holding onto these negative emotions only weighs us down and hinders our own healing and growth. Today, we seek your guidance and strength to let go of resentment and anger in our broken relationships.

Lord, we confess that carrying the weight of resentment and anger keeps us from experiencing the freedom and peace that you desire for us. We recognize that forgiveness is a choice—a choice to release the hold these negative emotions have on us and to surrender them to you. Grant us the courage to make that choice, Lord, and to trust in your power to bring healing and restoration.

Help us, Lord, to see others through your eyes of compassion and grace. Enable us to empathize with their weaknesses and struggles, recognizing that they too are in need of your love and forgiveness. Soften our hearts, Lord, and replace our resentment with empathy, our anger with understanding, and our hurt with compassion.

Teach us, Lord, to set healthy boundaries in our relationships, while still extending grace and forgiveness. Show us how to navigate difficult conversations with love and wisdom, seeking understanding rather than holding onto resentment. Give us the strength to release our grip on the past, to let go of grudges, and to choose forgiveness as a path to freedom.

Lord, we pray for the healing of our wounded hearts. Fill us with your love and peace, so that we may experience true restoration. Help us to forgive as you have forgiven us, knowing that forgiveness is not condoning the hurtful actions but releasing ourselves from thebondage of resentment and anger.

We acknowledge that forgiveness is a process, and it may take time to fully let go of the pain caused by broken relationships. But with your guidance, Lord, we can embark on this journey of healing and liberation. Grant us the strength to confront the wounds of the past, to face our emotions, and to surrender them to you.

As we release resentment and anger, we invite your Holy Spirit to fill the empty spaces in our hearts with your peace and love. Heal the scars left by broken relationships and restore our inner harmony. Help us to find healing not only for ourselves but also for those who have caused us pain.

In your infinite wisdom, you remind us that forgiveness does not mean forgetting or condoning the hurtful actions. Rather, it is a decision to relinquish our desire for revenge and to trust in your justice. We place our hurts, grievances, and the outcomes of broken relationships into your hands, knowing that you are the ultimate judge and healer.

Lord, we pray for the strength to resist the temptation of dwelling on past grievances. Grant us the grace to focus on the present and to cultivate a heart of forgiveness and reconciliation. Guide us in embracing a future filled with hope and restored relationships.

We also recognize that forgiveness is not only for the benefit of the other person but also for our own well-being. As we let go of resentment and anger, we open ourselves up to the possibility of healing and new beginnings. Help us to walk in the freedom that comes from forgiving, experiencing the joy and peace that can only come from you.

In your mercy, Lord, teach us to forgive ourselves for the mistakes we have made in relationships. Release us from the guilt and self-condemnation that weigh us down, and grant us the grace to learn from our past and grow into better versions of ourselves.

As we journey on the path of forgiveness, we pray for your guidance and strength. Empower us to extend forgiveness and seek reconciliation where possible. May our broken relationships become opportunities for growth, understanding, and the demonstration of your love and grace.

In the name of Jesus, the perfect example of forgiveness, we pray. Amen.

Prayer for Reconciliation and Restoration

Gracious God, we come before you with hearts longing for reconciliation and restoration in our broken relationships. We recognize that human connections can falter, causing pain and separation. Today, we humbly seek your divine intervention, believing in your power to heal and restore what has been lost.

Lord, you are the ultimate reconciler. We lift up to you the broken relationships in our lives, whether they are with family members, friends, colleagues, or acquaintances. We ask for your divine guidance and wisdom to navigate the path of reconciliation.

Grant us the humility to admit our own faults and shortcomings in these relationships. Help us to see our part in the breakdown and to take responsibility for our actions. Give us the strength to offer sincere apologies, seeking forgiveness from those we have hurt.

We pray for the individuals with whom we have broken relationships. Soften their hearts, Lord, and grant them the willingness to engage in dialogue and seek reconciliation. Remove any bitterness, pride, or barriers that hinder restoration. Work in their lives, even as you work in ours, to bring about healing and forgiveness.

Lord, we understand that reconciliation does not always mean the complete restoration of the relationship to what it once was. Sometimes, it means finding a new way forward—a path of understanding, respect, and healthy boundaries. Help us to discern what is best for each relationship and to seek reconciliation in a manner that honors you and respects the well-being of all parties involved.

We recognize that reconciliation requires patience and perseverance. It may take time, effort, and vulnerability to rebuild trust and restore the bond that was broken between us. Grant us the strength and determination to stay committed to the process, even when it feels challenging or uncertain.

Lord, as we embark on the journey of reconciliation, fill our hearts with your love and compassion. Give us the ability to extend grace and forgiveness, just as you have extended it to us. Help us to let go of resentment, anger, and past hurts, embracing a future of restored relationships.

We also pray for your divine intervention in situations where reconciliation may not be possible or safe. Protect us from toxic or abusive relationships and give us the wisdom to discern when it is necessary to walk away for our own well-being. Grant us the strength to set healthy boundaries and to find healing and peace in the midst of brokenness.

Lord, we surrender these broken relationships into your hands, trusting that you can bring beauty from ashes. We acknowledge that true reconciliation is a miracle that can only be accomplished through your grace and power. We invite you to work in and through us, transforming hearts and bringing about healing and restoration.

In the process of reconciliation, teach us valuable lessons about forgiveness, empathy, and unconditional love. Help us to grow in compassion and understanding towards others, recognizing that we are all imperfect and in need of your grace. May our broken relationships become opportunities for personal growth, humility, and the demonstration of your redemptive power.

We pray for the courage to take the necessary steps towards reconciliation, even when it feels uncomfortable or vulnerable. Equip us with the words to communicate our intentions and desires for restoration. Grant us the patience to listen with empathy and understanding, allowing space for healing conversations and heartfelt apologies.

Above all, Lord, may our pursuit of reconciliation reflect your love and bring glory to your name. May our transformed relationships become a testimony to your power and grace, inspiring others to seek healing and restoration in their own lives.

In the precious name of Jesus, our ultimate reconciler, we pray. Amen.

CHAPTER 7: PRAYERS FOR BUILDING HEALTHY COMMUNICATION

Prayer for Open and Honest Communication

Heavenly Father, we come before you with grateful hearts, recognizing that healthy communication is essential for building strong and thriving relationships. We acknowledge that effective communication requires openness, honesty, and vulnerability. Today, we humbly ask for your guidance as we seek to cultivate these qualities in our interactions with others.

Lord, help us to break down the barriers that hinder open communication. Remove any fear, pride, or insecurity that prevents us from expressing our thoughts, feelings, and needs honestly. Grant us the courage to share our hearts with sincerity, knowing that you are a God who listens and understands.

Teach us the importance of active listening, Lord. Help us to set aside distractions and truly engage with others when they speak. Grant us the ability to listen not only to their words but also to their emotions, desires, and concerns. May we be present and attentive, showing genuine care and empathy.

Lord, we ask for your wisdom in choosing our words wisely. Guide us to speak with kindness, respect, and clarity. May our words build up and encourage others, rather than tear them down. Give us the discernment to know when to speak and when to remain silent, understanding that sometimes silence can be a powerful form of communication.

In our interactions, Lord, help us to be mindful of the impact our words may have on others. May we be sensitive to their feelings and experiences, seeking to understand their perspectives without judgment or defensiveness. Grant us the humility to admit when we are wrong and the willingness to apologize and seek forgiveness.

Lord, we invite your Holy Spirit to guide our conversations. Fill us with your love and grace, so that our words may reflect your character. May our communication be marked by patience, gentleness, and self-control. Help us to express our thoughts and emotions in a way that fosters understanding and unity.

In situations where communication has broken down or become strained, we pray for your intervention, Lord. Heal any misunderstandings, restore trust, and mend broken bonds. Grant us the wisdom to seek reconciliation and to actively work towards rebuilding healthy communication.

Lord, we commit our relationships and communication into your hands. May you be the foundation of our interactions, guiding us in love and truth. Empower us to create an atmosphere of open and honest communication, where trust and understanding can flourish.

We offer this prayer in the name of Jesus, who is the perfect example of loving and effective communication. Amen.

Prayer for Listening and Understanding

Gracious Lord, we come before you knowing that communication is not only about speaking but also about listening and understanding. We recognize that listening is an act of love and respect, and it is vital for building healthy and meaningful relationships. Today, we humbly ask for your guidance as we seek to become better listeners.

Help us, Lord, to quiet our hearts and minds, enabling us to truly hear others when they speak. Remove the distractions that hinder our ability to listen attentively. Grant us the discipline to set aside our own thoughts, agendas, and biases, and to fully engage in the conversation at hand.

Teach us to listen not only with our ears but also with our hearts. Help us to discern the emotions, needs, and desires behind the words spoken. May we be sensitive to the non-verbal cues and body language that can reveal deeper meanings. Give us the empathy to understand the perspectives of others, even if they differ from our own.

Lord, we confess that sometimes we are quick to interrupt, offer advice, or jump to conclusions while listening. Forgive us for these tendencies and help us to cultivate patience and self-control. Grant us the wisdom to know when to speak and when to remain silent, understanding that sometimes the greatest act of listening is to give others the space to share without interruption or judgment.

Holy Spirit, guide us in active listening. Help us to ask thoughtful questions that invite deeper understanding. Give us the ability to reflect back what we have heard, demonstrating that we value and respect the other person's perspective. May our listening be a source of comfort, validation, and support for those who entrust their thoughts and feelings to us.

Lord, we also recognize that true understanding goes beyond the words spoken. Help us to listen with discernment, perceiving the underlying needs and desires of others. Grant us the ability to empathize with their experiences, joys, and pains. May our listening foster connection and create a safe space for vulnerability and authenticity.

In our relationships, Lord, we pray for the humility to admit when we have misunderstood or misinterpreted. Help us to approach conversations with a willingness to learn and grow. Give us the courage to ask for clarification and to seek reconciliation when misunderstandings arise. May our commitment to listening and understanding strengthen our bonds and deepen our connections.

Lord, we acknowledge that listening and understanding require patience and intentionality. We confess that at times we are too quick to jump to conclusions or make assumptions. Help us to suspend judgment and approach each conversation with an open mind and a humble heart. Grant us the grace to withhold our own agendas and biases, allowing space for diverse perspectives to be heard and valued.

Finally, Lord, we recognize that you are the ultimate listener and understander. You know our deepest thoughts, desires, and longings. Help us to seek your wisdom and guidance in our communication. May our interactions reflect your love and grace, and may they bring honor to your name.

In the name of Jesus, our perfect example of listening and understanding, we pray. Amen.

Prayer for Resolving Conflicts with Love and Grace

Heavenly Father, we come before you recognizing that conflicts and disagreements are a natural part of relationships. However, we also acknowledge that conflicts can cause division and strain if not handled with love and grace. Today, we lift up our conflicts to you and ask for your guidance and intervention in resolving them.

Lord, when conflicts arise, help us to approach them

with humility and a desire for reconciliation. Grant us the wisdom to address the issues at hand with clarity and honesty, while still maintaining a spirit of love and respect. May our words and actions reflect your grace and peace.

In moments of conflict, Lord, we pray for self-control and patience. Help us to manage our emotions and to refrain from responding in anger or defensiveness. Give us the ability to listen attentively, seeking to understand the concerns and perspectives of others. May our communication be characterized by empathy and compassion.

Lord, in the midst of conflicts, we ask for your guidance in finding common ground and seeking solutions that honor the needs and well-being of all involved. Grant us the wisdom to compromise when necessary and the courage to stand firm when it is in the best interest of the relationship. Help us to prioritize unity and reconciliation over being right.

We also pray for the strength and humility to admit when we are wrong or have contributed to the conflict. Teach us to take responsibility for our actions and words, and to offer sincere apologies and seek forgiveness when needed. May our willingness to humble ourselves pave the way for healing and restoration.

Lord, we invite your Holy Spirit to be present in our conflicts, serving as a mediator and a source of wisdom. Help us to communicate with gentleness and grace, even when the conversation becomes difficult or tense. Grant us the ability to speak truth in love, offering constructive feedback and seeking understanding.

In moments when resolution seems challenging or impossible, we surrender our conflicts into your hands, Lord. We trust that you can bring beauty from ashes and reconciliation from brokenness. Give us the patience to wait upon you and to allow your perfect timing in the process of resolution. Help us to persevere in seeking reconciliation, even when it feels difficult or discouraging.

Lord, we also recognize that conflicts can reveal areas where growth and change are needed within ourselves. Grant us the humility to examine our own hearts and attitudes, and to be willing to make the necessary adjustments for the sake of peace and unity. May our conflicts become opportunities for personal growth and transformation.

Finally, Lord, we lift up all the conflicts and broken

relationships that weigh heavy on our hearts. We ask for your healing touch and restoration. Soften hardened hearts, mend broken bonds, and bring reconciliation where there is division. May your love and grace prevail in every relationship, bringing about lasting harmony and unity.

We entrust all these prayers to you, knowing that you are the God of reconciliation and restoration. In the name of Jesus, our ultimate peacemaker, we pray. Amen.

CHAPTER 8: PRAYERS FOR STRENGTHENING PARENTING SKILLS

Prayer for Patience and Wisdom in Parenting

Heavenly Father, we come before you as parents, recognizing the immense responsibility and privilege it is to raise children. We acknowledge that parenting can be both joyful and challenging, and we need your wisdom and strength to navigate this journey. Today, we humbly ask for your guidance in developing patience and wisdom as we fulfill our role as parents.

Lord, parenting requires a great deal of patience, as we are constantly faced with the demands and needs of our children. Grant us the ability to respond with grace and gentleness, even in moments of frustration or exhaustion. Help us to understand that patience is not simply waiting, but it is a posture of love and endurance that reflects your character.

We also seek your wisdom, Lord, as we make decisions and choices that impact our children's lives. Give us discernment to know how to guide them in the right path. May your wisdom permeate our thoughts and actions, so that we may lead with integrity and righteousness. Grant us the insight to see beyond the immediate circumstances and to consider the long-term effects of our parenting choices.

Lord, in moments when we feel inadequate or unsure, remind us that we are not alone in this journey. Your Holy Spirit is our ever-present helper and guide. Help us to rely on you for wisdom, strength, and understanding. May your Spirit lead us in every aspect of our parenting, from discipline to encouragement, from teaching to listening.

We also pray for wisdom in setting boundaries and providing discipline for our children. Grant us the ability to discipline with love, setting clear expectations and consequences while still showing them grace and forgiveness. May our discipline be rooted in a desire to teach and guide our children towards maturity and godliness.

Lord, we recognize that our own patience and wisdom are limited. Help us to rely on you and to seek your wisdom through prayer and the study of your Word. Fill us with the knowledge of your will, so that we may parent according to your divine plan. May our children see your love and wisdom reflected in our lives and may it have a lasting impact on their own journey of faith.

We commit ourselves and our parenting journey to you, Lord. Strengthen us in times of weakness, encourage us in times of doubt, and guide us in every decision we make. May our parenting be a reflection of your love and grace, pointing our children to you.

In the name of Jesus, who is the perfect example of patience and wisdom, we pray. Amen.

Prayer for Nurturing a Healthy Parent-Child Relationship

Heavenly Father, we come before you with grateful hearts for the gift of parenthood and the privilege of nurturing a healthy parent-child relationship. We acknowledge that the bond between parents and children is a sacred one, designed by you for mutual love, support, and growth. Today, we seek your guidance and blessings as we strive to foster a strong and nurturing connection with our children.

Lord, help us to cultivate an environment of love, acceptance, and understanding within our family. Grant us the ability to create a safe space where our children feel valued, heard, and respected. May our words and actions reflect your unconditional love, so that they may experience your love through our relationship with them.

Teach us to listen attentively to our children, Lord. Help us to be present and engaged, giving them our full attention when they speak. May we create opportunities for open and honest communication, where they can freely express their thoughts, feelings, and concerns. Give us the wisdom to respond with empathy, compassion, and understanding.

Lord, we also pray for wisdom in nurturing healthy boundaries and discipline. Guide us to set appropriate limits that promote their safety, well-being, and character development. Help us to discipline with grace and love and to correct our children in a way that builds them up rather than tearing them down. Give us the discernment to know when to be firm and when to extend grace, always seeking their best interests and long-term growth.

Father, we recognize that our role as parents extends beyond simply meeting their physical needs. We desire to nurture their emotional, mental, and spiritual well-being as well. Grant us the wisdom to provide emotional support, to encourage their growth and independence, and to instill in them a sense of worth and identity rooted in you.

Lord, we also pray for humility in our parenting journey. Help us to recognize our own shortcomings and to acknowledge when we make mistakes. Give us the humility to ask for forgiveness from our children when we fall short, modeling grace and accountability. May our vulnerability and willingness to learn and grow inspire them to do the same.

In moments of conflict or disagreement, Lord, we ask for your guidance and wisdom. Help us to navigate challenging situations with patience, understanding, and empathy. Give us the ability to seek resolution and reconciliation, fostering a spirit of unity within our family. May our interactions with our children be characterized by love, respect, and grace.

Lord, we entrust our children into your loving care. We recognize that ultimately, they belong to you, and you have entrusted them to our stewardship. Help us to be faithful in raising them to love and serve you.

Guide us in teaching them your ways and your truth, that they may grow into men and women of godly character.

We pray for your strength and resilience in our parenting journey, Lord. Grant us the energy, patience, and endurance we need to fulfill our responsibilities with joy and perseverance. Fill us with your Holy Spirit, empowering us to be the parents you have called us to be.

In the name of Jesus, our perfect example of love and nurturing, we pray. Amen.

Prayer for Guidance and Strength in Parenting Challenges

Heavenly Father, we come before you today, acknowledging that parenting is not without its challenges. We recognize that there will be times of difficulty, uncertainty, and adversity along this journey. In those moments, we seek your guidance and strength to navigate the parenting challenges we face.

Lord, you are the source of all wisdom and understanding. We ask for your guidance as we encounter various situations and decisions in our parenting roles. Give us the discernment to make choices that align with your will and are in the best interest of our children. Help us to see beyond the immediate circumstances and consider the long-term effects of our actions and choices.

When we face moments of doubt and uncertainty, Lord, grant us the clarity and peace of mind to trust in your provision. Help us to lean on you for wisdom and strength, knowing that you are our ever-present help in times of need. May we find solace and confidence in your unfailing love and faithfulness.

Father, we pray for patience and endurance when the challenges seem overwhelming. Parenting can be demanding, both physically and emotionally. Give us the strength to persevere during sleepless nights, tantrums, rebellious phases, and the many ups and downs that come with raising children. May your grace sustain us, enabling us to respond with love and patience even in the most trying circumstances.

Lord, we also ask for humility and a teachable spirit as parents. Help us to recognize our own limitations and areas where we need growth. Give us the courage to seek guidance and support from others who can offer wisdom and perspective. May we be willing to learn from our mistakes and continually grow in our understanding of effective parenting.

In moments of frustration or feeling overwhelmed, remind us of the power of prayer. Teach us to bring our concerns, worries, and challenges before you, knowing that you hear our prayers and are attentive to our cries. Strengthen our faith as we trust in your provision and rely on your guidance.

Lord, we pray for unity and cooperation between parents as we navigate the challenges together. Help us to communicate effectively, to support one another, and to work as a team in our parenting efforts. May our relationship be a source of strength and stability for our children.

Finally, we lift up our children to you, Lord. We pray for their well-being, their growth, and their resilience. Protect them from harm, surround them with your love, and guide them along the paths you have prepared for them. May our parenting be a reflection of your grace and love, pointing our children to your truth and leading them closer to you.

In the name of Jesus, who understands the challenges of parenthood and offers us his strength, we pray. Amen.

CHAPTER 9: PRAYERS FOR BLENDED FAMILIES

Prayer for Unity and Harmony in Blended Families

Heavenly Father, we come before you today, lifting up blended families to your loving care. We recognize that blending two families together can bring unique challenges and complexities. In these moments, we seek your guidance and intervention to foster unity and harmony within our blended families.

Lord, we pray for unity among all family members. Help us to build strong bonds and create a sense of togetherness as we navigate the blending of our lives. May our hearts be open to accepting and embracing one another, recognizing that we are all part of this new family unit. Give us the willingness to let go of past hurts, resentments, and differences, and instead, cultivate an environment of love, understanding, and respect.

Father, we ask for your wisdom and discernment as we navigate the dynamics of blended families. Help us to understand the unique needs and challenges that arise when blending different backgrounds, traditions, and parenting styles. Guide us in making decisions that promote the well-being and happiness of all family members. Grant us the patience and understanding to work through conflicts and differences in a manner that builds bridges and fosters growth.

Lord, we pray for love and acceptance to abound within our blended families. Help us to create an environment where each family member feels valued, loved, and included. May we extend grace, forgiveness, and compassion to one another, recognizing that we are all on this journey together. Help us to celebrate our differences and embrace the richness that each individual brings to our family.

In the midst of the challenges that can arise in blended families, we lean on your strength and guidance, Lord. Give us the perseverance and resilience to navigate the complexities and uncertainties with grace and patience. Help us to seek your wisdom and counsel in every decision and interaction. May your Holy Spirit lead us and empower us to build strong and loving relationships within our blended family.

Father, we also lift up any children involved in our blended family. Grant them a sense of security and belonging. Help them to adapt to the changes and transitions that come with blending families. Fill their hearts with your love and peace, reassuring them that they are cherished and valued by each member of the family.

Lord, we acknowledge that blending families requires ongoing effort and commitment. We pray for strength and determination to persevere through the challenges and to continually nurture our relationships. May our blended family be a reflection of your love and grace, a testament to the power of healing and restoration.

In the name of Jesus, who unites and transforms us, we pray. Amen.

Prayer for Love and Acceptance among Stepfamily Members

Gracious Lord, we come before you today, seeking your guidance and blessing upon our stepfamily. We acknowledge that blending families brings together individuals from different backgrounds and experiences. We recognize the importance of cultivating love and acceptance among all stepfamily members.

Father, we ask for your grace to fill our hearts and enable us to extend love and acceptance to one another. Help us to see each family member through your eyes, valuing their unique contributions and embracing their differences. Teach us to be patient, understanding, and compassionate as we navigate the intricacies of our stepfamily dynamics.

Lord, we pray for healing in any wounds or hurts that may exist within our stepfamily. Heal any resentments, bitterness, or misunderstandings that have arisen from past experiences. Grant us the strength to forgive and release any negative emotions, replacing them with a spirit of reconciliation and harmony. May our stepfamily be a place of healing and restoration.

We ask for your guidance, Father, in building strong

and loving relationships within our stepfamily. Help us to communicate openly and honestly, fostering a spirit of trust and vulnerability. Give us the wisdom to navigate the unique challenges that arise, such as different parenting styles, conflicting loyalties, and establishing new roles and boundaries. Grant us the discernment to address these challenges with grace and understanding.

Lord, we pray for the children in our stepfamily. Give them a sense of belonging and security as they navigate the complexities of blending families. Help them to adjust to new family dynamics and build strong connections with their stepsiblings and stepparents. May they feel loved, accepted, and valued within our stepfamily.

Father, we seek your guidance in fostering a spirit of cooperation and unity among all stepfamily members. Help us to work together as a team, supporting and encouraging one another. Give us the wisdom to make decisions that prioritize the well-being and happiness of all family members. Strengthen the bonds of love within our stepfamily, creating a supportive and nurturing environment for everyone involved.

Lord, we pray for patience and understanding in

times of conflict or disagreement. Teach us to resolve conflicts peacefully and with respect, seeking reconciliation and understanding. Grant us the humility to admit our mistakes and the willingness to forgive one another. May our stepfamily be characterized by grace and a willingness to work through challenges together.

We lift up our stepfamily to you, Lord, knowing that you are the ultimate source of love and unity. Help us to rely on your strength and guidance as we navigate the joys and struggles of blending families. Pour out your blessings upon our stepfamily, filling our home with peace, love, and harmony.

In the name of Jesus, who unites us as one family in your Kingdom, we pray. Amen.

Prayer for Strength and Guidance in Navigating the Challenges of Blended Families

Heavenly Father, we come before you with humble hearts, seeking your strength and guidance as we navigate the unique challenges that come with being part of a blended family. We recognize that blending families requires patience, understanding, and a reliance on your wisdom and grace.

Lord, we ask for your strength to sustain us during difficult moments. Grant us the endurance to persevere through the adjustments and transitions that arise as we blend our lives together. Give us the resilience to face the complexities and uncertainties with unwavering faith in your provision.

Father, we acknowledge that blending families can bring forth feelings of insecurity, fear, and doubt. We pray for your guidance in overcoming these challenges. Help us to trust in your divine plan for our blended family and to find solace in your unwavering love and faithfulness. Guide us in making decisions that promote unity, understanding, and harmony within our family.

Lord, we pray for wisdom in navigating the different roles and responsibilities that come with blending families. Help us to establish healthy boundaries and clear communication channels. Grant us the discernment to balance the needs and desires of each family member, fostering an environment of mutual respect and support.

As we blend our traditions, routines, and values, Lord, we ask for your grace to help us find common ground. May our shared experiences and celebrations become moments of joy and connection. Give us the wisdom to honor and appreciate the unique backgrounds and perspectives that each family member brings, fostering a sense of belonging and acceptance.

Father, we lift up our children to you, knowing that their well-being is of utmost importance. Grant them strength and resilience as they adapt to the changes and dynamics of our blended family. Help us, as parents and stepparents, to provide a nurturing and loving environment where they can thrive and grow. Guide us in building strong relationships with our stepchildren, rooted in love, understanding, and mutual respect.

Lord, we also ask for your grace and wisdom in navigating relationships with former spouses or partners. Help us to show grace and kindness, even in moments of tension or disagreement. Grant us the humility to put the best interests of our children first, seeking cooperative and respectful co-parenting relationships.

Finally, Father, we pray for your divine intervention in healing any wounds or conflicts within our blended family. Soften hardened hearts, mend broken relationships, and restore harmony and peace. May our blended family be a testament to your transforming power and the beauty that can arise from unity in diversity.

In the name of Jesus, who understands the challenges of family dynamics and offers us his love and grace, we pray. Amen.

CONCLUSION

Embracing Love, Harmony, and Lasting Connections

As we come to the conclusion of this book, "Prayers for Strengthening Relationships and Family: Nurturing Love, Restoring Harmony, and Building Lasting Connections," we reflect on the transformative power of prayer in our relationships. Throughout these chapters, we have explored various aspects of family dynamics and sought divine guidance in nurturing love, restoring harmony, and building lasting connections within our families.

In a world where relationships can face numerous challenges, it is essential to recognize the importance of investing in our family bonds. The journey of strengthening relationships and fostering a sense of belonging requires intentional effort, patience, and reliance on the power of prayer. It is through prayer that we invite God's presence into our lives, seeking His wisdom, love, and grace to guide us in our interactions with our loved ones.

Throughout this book, we have offered prayers for spousal bonds, parent-child relationships, sibling connections, extended families, friendships, healing broken relationships, building healthy communication, strengthening parenting skills, navigating blended families, and growing in love and understanding. Each prayer is a testament to our deep desire to cultivate strong, loving, and harmonious relationships within our families.

As we conclude, we encourage you to continue to pray for your relationships and family, knowing that God is faithful to hear and answer our prayers according to His perfect will. May these prayers serve as a foundation for your own conversations with God, allowing you to pour out your heart, seek His guidance, and experience His transforming power in your relationships.

Remember that the journey of nurturing relationships and building lasting connections is a lifelong endeavor. It requires patience, forgiveness, and a commitment to love unconditionally. May the prayers in this book serve as a source of inspiration, encouragement, and support as you navigate the joys and challenges of family life.

Finally, we offer this final prayer of blessing:

Heavenly Father, we thank you for the opportunity to journey through this book together, seeking your guidance and blessings upon our relationships and family. We pray that you would continue to pour out your love, grace, and wisdom upon us. May the words we have read and the prayers we have shared be seeds that grow and bear fruit in our lives.

Lord, we ask for your continued presence in our relationships, that you would strengthen the bonds of love, restore harmony where there is discord, and build lasting connections that are grounded in your love. May our families be a reflection of your unconditional love and grace, shining as a light in the world.

We pray for all the families represented by those who have read this book, that they would experience your transformative power in their lives. May they be filled with love, joy, and peace, and may their relationships be a source of strength and support.

In the name of Jesus, who taught us the importance of love and unity, we offer this prayer. Amen.

May you continue to embrace love, nurture relationships, and experience the blessings of a strengthened family. May your journey be filled with moments of joy, growth, and deepening connections.

Milton Keynes UK
Ingram Content Group UK Ltd.
UKHW020904291124
451807UK00013B/728